£7.99

A Pillar Box Red Publication

© 2010. Published by Pillar Box Red Publishing Ltd.

ISBN: 978-1-907823-05-3

we love you...

N-DUBZ

An Unauthorised 2011 Annual

Written by Martin Johnston
Designed by Chris Dalrymple

CONTENTS

08-09	We Love You N-Dubz Because…	20-21	Spotlight on Tulisa
10-11	What's on the N-Dubz iPod?	22	What's on the Menu?
12-13	Awards Galore!	23	Wordsearch
14-15	Spotlight on Fazer	26-27	10 Things You Didn't Know About N-Dubz!
16	Spot the Difference	28-29	N-Dubz: How it all Started
17	The Big Quiz	30-31	Spotlight on Danny
18-19	Best Mates		

34	All the Tunes: The Singles	50-51	Fierce! Tulisa's Style
36-37	Tulisa the Footie Star!	52-53	All the Tunes: The Albums
38-39	The A-Z of N-Dubz	54-55	Uncle B: The Man, The Album
40-41	Love For My Slum!	56	Street Smart! Fazer's Style
44-45	Dappy: Hat's Magic!	57	Street Smart! Dappy's Style
46-47	N-Dubz & War Child	58-59	Video Starz!
48	Name That Tune	60-61	Answers

we *love* you...

N-Dubz because...

...there are so many big tunes!

...fazer's so cool!

...n-dubz fans have their own name, 'n-dublets'

...n-dubz fans have their own language, duku yourself!

...the video for 'ouch' has had 9 million hits on youtube. boom!

...you're 4 real!

...dappy's unique!

...tulisa's so stylish!

TUNE! WHAT'S ON THE N-DUBZ iPOD?

What tunes do you think are on the N-Dubz iPod for keeps? These are some of the artists that influenced their sound:

iPod

N-Dubz

- Elvis
- Aretha Franklin
- John Lee Hooker
- Billie Holiday
- Wu-Tang Clan
- Phil Collins
- Eminem
- Nas
- Tupac
- Drake
- Boyz II Men
- Monica
- Aaliyah

FAZER

Early on it was Aretha Franklin, John Lee Hooker, Billie Holiday, Elvis and Motown. But it's really all about the Hip Hop for Fazer, especially '36 Chambers' by Wu-Tang Clan.

TULISA

As a young girl it was older R&B, Boyz II Men and Monica. But Aaliyah's 'One in a Million' really stands out.

DAPPY

Reckons Phil Collins is one of the best all-round musicians in the world! And he loves the lyrics of Eminem, Nas, Tupac and a Canadian rapper called Drake.

AWARDS GALORE!

Even though they've only been on the scene for a few years, N-Dubz have already earned the respect of the music business and racked up some serious awards.

2007
MOBO Awards
Best UK Newcomers: Won!

2008
Urban Music Awards
Best Group: Nominated
Best Music Video for 'Ouch': Nominated

2009
O₂ Silver Clef Awards – Digital Award: Won!

2009
MOBO Awards
Best UK Act: Won!
Best Album for 'Uncle B': Won!

2010
BRIT Awards
Best British Single for 'Number 1': Nominated

13

SPOTLIGHT ON FAZER

Real name: Richard Rawson.

Role in N-Dubz: Spittin' lyrics, rapping, producing.

N-Dubz name: Fazer.

Why: He loves motorbikes and used to borrow his mate's super-fast Yamaha Fazer.

Birthday: 5th February 1987.

Star sign: Aquarius.

Born in: Camden, London.

Early days: Fazer first met Dappy when they were both young kids at a local karate class. They became best friends at Haverstock School in London and they started writing and rapping together when they were 11 years old.

Did you know? He appeared as a dancer in a video for the K.I.G song "Head, Shoulders, Kneez and Toez".

SPOT THE DIFFERENCE

Look at these two photos of N-Dubz.
Can you spot the 6 differences between them?

THE BIG QUIZ

1. What is Fazer's real name?
Richard rawson.

2. What is N-Dubz's second album called?
against all odds

3. How many MOBO awards have N-Dubz won so far?
three

4. Dappy's Dad, Byron, was in 1970's hit group Mungo Jerry. True or false? *true*

5. What famous US hip hop record label signed N-Dubz in 2010?
def Jam

6. Who got to the top of the charts with 'Number 1' featuring N-Dubz? *Tinchy Stryder*

7. What is Tulisa's real first name?
tula

8. The postcode of what area of London gave N-Dubz their name?
Camden

9. The group's original name was 'Lickle Pinchers'. True or false?
false it was "Lickle Rinsers crew"

10. In what year did N-Dubz win the MOBO award for the best UK newcomer? *2007*

11. Dappy and Tulisa's surname is Contostavlos. True or false?
true

12. What is the name of the character played by Tulisa in the TV series Dubplate Drama? *Laurissa*

13. What character does Dappy play in the same series (see Q12)?
Sleezy

14. N-Dubz's first album is called 'Uncle B'. True or false?
true

15. What was the title of the reality TV show on 4Music following the band? *Dubplate drama*

16. Which British newspaper called N-Dubz "Britain's number 1 Band" in 2009? *the sun*

17. What film did the song 'We Dance On' feature in?
street dance 3d

18. In what year did N-Dubz win the MOBO award for best UK act?
2009

19. What is the name of the N-Dubz single featuring Mr. Hudson?
Playing with fire

20. What is Dappy's real first name?
dino

Answers on page 60/61

BEST MATES

SKEPTA_ GARY BARLOW

tinchy stryder Mr Hudson CHIPMUNK

Collaborate and listen! N-Dubz make sure they keep their sound fresh and exciting by working with some of the best musicians and producers in the business.

The first official release to have credited anyone but Dappy, Fazer or Tulisa was the single 'Ouch', which had 4 remixes included on the B-side: a 'Full Club' and a 'Bassline' mix by The Wideboys, plus remixes by Martin K and Jorg Schmidt of N-Force.

The first time they featured on someone else's track was Tinchy Stryder's 'Number 1', which

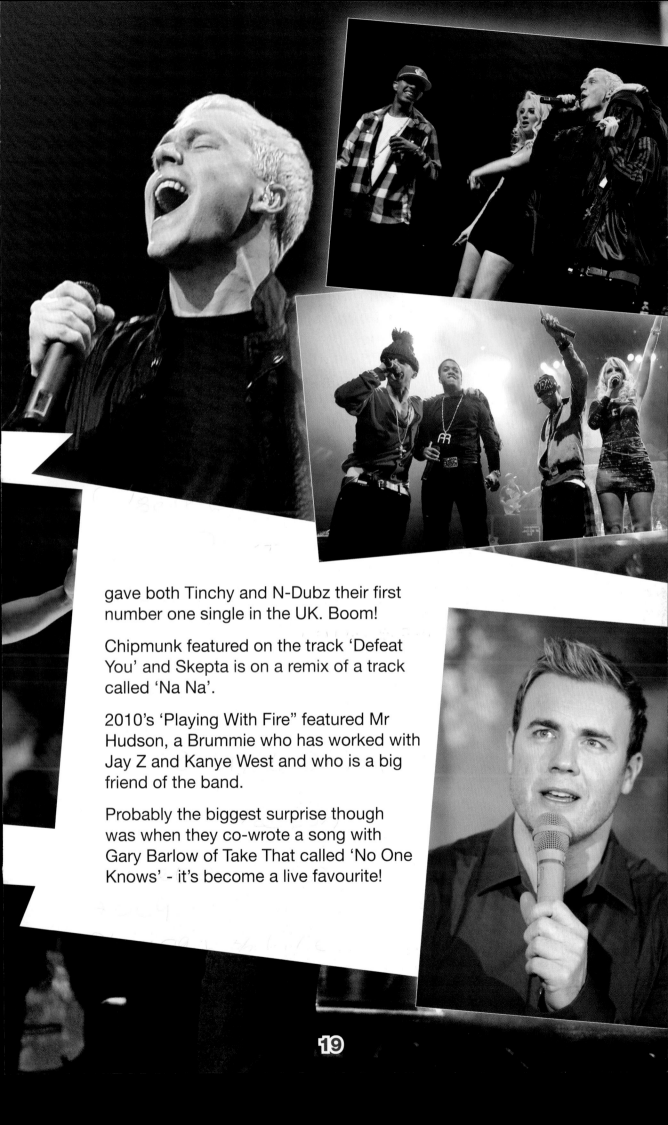

gave both Tinchy and N-Dubz their first number one single in the UK. Boom!

Chipmunk featured on the track 'Defeat You' and Skepta is on a remix of a track called 'Na Na'.

2010's 'Playing With Fire" featured Mr Hudson, a Brummie who has worked with Jay Z and Kanye West and who is a big friend of the band.

Probably the biggest surprise though was when they co-wrote a song with Gary Barlow of Take That called 'No One Knows' - it's become a live favourite!

SPOTLIGHT ON TULISA

Real full name: Tula Paulinea Contostavlos.

Role in N-Dubz: Singer, songwriter, mother hen!

N-Dubz name: Tulisa.

Why: It's just a stage name that sounds better…

Birthday: 13th July 1988.

Star sign: Cancer.

Born in: Camden, London.

Early days: Young Tula had a very difficult childhood, changing schools many times and caring for her sick mother. However when she was 12 she moved to the same school as her cousin Dappy where she was much happier. She joined him and Fazer in their new group and N-Dubz was born.

Did you know? Tulisa is one of the stars of the TV show 'Dubplate Drama'. She plays Laurissa who is a singer in a band!

21

What's on the Menu?

It's the big question that every N-Dublet wants to know. What's the fuel behind N-Dubz?

As Kids

Just like most kids, Dappy and Fazer both loved Kentucky Fried Chicken when they were young. Not just for the food but for hanging out too!

At School

Dappy…casserole with chips!
Tulisa…chicken burger!

Fazer…chocolate cake with chocolate custard

These Days

Before they go on stage N-Dubz like a selection of Red Bull (but not too much!), Capri Sun, white wine, Twiglets, fish and chips (and salad!) and plenty of chocolate bars.

WORDSEARCH

Here's a wicked wordsearch for you! Find the 18 words or phrases linked to N-Dubz!

```
C Q Q F F L C H C U O N N P Q
M R N R T B V K K T N B G T T
T A F L U J Y C Q L R L L Y B
R L J Z L K Z R X C Y T P X M
S K K F A M U L O T U L I S A
T W R N E Z K K N N P W N E G
E K L F W D U B V B H Y N Z N
L C N T K H D K M I P O X N L
B D K D I N O R P P R Y E D J
U R F J Y U R H A E M D L T R
D K L A N K O D B L M M Z D A
N V N C Z P N M L A M G M M P
V G L M B E U I C B M K J O A
K E P B N N R X P G K N Y B P
B Q C Q Y J N O D N O L Q O N
```

duku   camden   dino

dappy   byron   tula

tulisa

fazer   hip hop   london

mobo   uncle B   number one

pinky   papa   def jam

ouch

ndublets

Solution on page 60/61

10 Things You Didn't Know About N-Dubz!

Think you know everything about Dappy & co? Here's ten things we bet you never knew!

1 Dappy is rumoured to have a habit of buying and crashing model planes.

2 Fazer used to run for Camden, his speciality was the 1500m.

3 N-Dubz's first ever video 'Every Day Of My Life' only cost £500 to make.

4 The N-Dubz MySpace site had over 10 million hits in 2009.

5 N-Dubz call a £50 note a 'pinky'.

6 The boys usually have a barber backstage at every show.

7 Their backstage rider (the list of stuff they need in the dressing room) includes Nando's chicken, Twiglets, Capri Sun and Red Bull.

8 As a youngster Fazer worked on a flower stall at Camden Market.

9 One of Tulisa's first jobs was at a music management company that handled The Who and Led Zeppelin.

10 Dappy's favourite holiday activity is jet-skiing in Barbados.

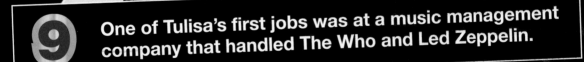

Have you heard of the 'Lickle Rinsers Crew'? Yeah? Then duku yourself! That's what N-Dubz called themselves when they first started laying down tracks.

Dappy and Fazer first met when they tussled as kids at a local karate club in North London. But they didn't start rolling together until they met again as 12 year olds at Haverstock School in Camden.

They soon found they could both spit a few lyrics and started to clash. By the time they were 13 they felt ready to make records. Dappy's dad, Byron, had a studio and they went there with a guy called DJ Deekline to record a track.

The only problem was they wanted a singer, a solid female voice. Dappy knew his cousin Tula wanted to sing but initially she turned the boys down because she wanted to be a solo performer, even though she was only 11!

But eventually they got it together and took their first steps in the recording industry as the Lickle Rinsers Crew with a track called "What Is This World Coming To?" The rest is N-Dubz history!

N-DUBZ
How it all started

SPOTLIGHT ON DAPPY

Real full name: Costas Dinos Contostavlos.

Role in N-Dubz: Lyricist, MC, rapper, producer.

N-Dubz name: Dappy.

Why: He's a dapper gentleman!

Birthday: 11th June 1987.

Star sign: Gemini.

Born in: Camden, London.

Early days: Dino grew up in Camden and went to many local schools like St. Aloysius. He met Fazer at Haverstock School and they started rapping and writing together.

Did you know? Dappy has released two mixtapes called 'D to the A to the Ps to the Y' and 'Hot off These Streets' which feature artists like Frisco, Chipmunk, Wiley, Scorcher, Wizzy Wow and Tempa T.

ALL THE TUNES: THE SINGLES

You probably know that every N-Dubz single has made the top twenty, but can you name them all? They're all here...

Year	Title	UK Singles Chart - Highest Position	UK R&B Chart - Highest Position
2006	You Better Not Waste My Time	26	06
2006	I Swear	91	-
2007	Feva Las Vegas	57	11
2008	Ouch	22	03
2008	Papa, Can You Hear Me?	19	05
2009	Strong Again	24	07
2009	Wouldn't You	64	15
2009	I Need You	05	01
2010	Playing with Fire (Featuring Mr. Hudson)	14	03
2010	Say It's Over	40	10
2010	We Dance On (Featuring Bodyrox)	06	05

TULISA
THE FOOTIE STAR!

You probably know that Dappy loves his footie and is a big Arsenal fan.

But did you know Tulisa is a good player?

The whole band took part in the charity Soccer Sixes event in 2010 which was held at Charlton Athletic's Valley Stadium to raise money for the Samaritans.

While Dappy and Fazer's team did OK in the men's competition, Tulisa captained her women's team and won the tournament!

Tulisa had other celebrities like former Mis-teeq singer Su-Elise Nash, Hollyoaks actress Sasha Emmanuel and TV presenter Liv Boeree on her team. They beat two other teams which included Stacey Solomon from X Factor, The Cheeky Girls and Bianca Gascoigne.

She tweeted later: 'Yeeeeeeessss N-Dubz gals team won Soccer Six. As team captain

I'm taking home the trophy.
Told you we will defeat you.'

Not content with that Tulisa
then dolled herself up, curled
her hair and dashed off to
Wembley for a visit to some
live filming of an episode of
Britain's Got Talent!

THE A-Z OF N-DUBZ

A   is for **Aaliyah, a big influence on Tulisa.**

B   is for **Byron, forever!**

C   is for **Camden, the N-Dubz hood.**

D   is for **Dappy.**

E   is for **Eminem, another big influence.**

F   is for **Fazer.**

G   is for **Gary Barlow, friend and collaborator.**

H   is for **Mr Hudson, ditto!**

I   is for **'I swear'.**

J   is for **Jez Welham, the first DJ to back N-Dubz on radio.**

K   is for **Karate - how Dappy and Fazer first met.**

L   is for **Laurissa, T's character in 'Dubplate Drama'.**

M   is for **McCoys crisps, always in the rider.**

N is for North which is where the N of N-Dubz comes from.

O is for 'Ouch', of course.

P is for 'Papa, can you hear me?'

Q is for Queen, still listened to by Fazer.

R is for R&B.

S is for 'Strong Again' and 'Say it's over'.

T is for Tulisa, Tula and sometimes just 'T'!

U is for Uncle B.

V is for Vocalist, three of the best in N-Dubz!

W is for 'What is the world coming to?' - the song that started it all.

X is for Xbox, one of the ways Fazer likes to chill.

Y is for 'You better not waste my time'.

Z is for the last letter of the alphabet and the last letter of N-Dubz!

Kentish Town West

Belsize Park

Chalk Farm

✝ Camden Town

Town   Road

Caledonian Road

Camden Road

Caledonian

LOVE FOR MY SLUM!

One of Dappy and Fazer's early tunes was a song called Love For My Slum!

We all know that they are proud Londoners and that their hood is Camden but what do you know about NW1 – the postcode that gave N-Dubz their name?

NW1 is the postcode for Camden, Regent's Park and St. Pancras.

Regent's Park is home to the world famous London Zoo and St. Pancras has the Eurostar Rail Terminal. You can be in Paris from there in just over 3 hours!

As well as the trendy Lock area and it's wicked market (where we reckon Dappy picked up his first 'Dappy Hat'!) Camden has lots of top music venues.

N-Dubz have played the Roundhouse a few times but there's also The Electric Ballroom, Koko and The Dublin Castle, where many famous bands played early gigs.

NW1! Na Na!

DAPPY: HAT'S MAGIC!

D to the A to the Ps to the Y!

He's the dapper dude who's nearly as well known for his hats as for spittin' lyrics and writing killer tunes.

Here are just some of our favourites!

45

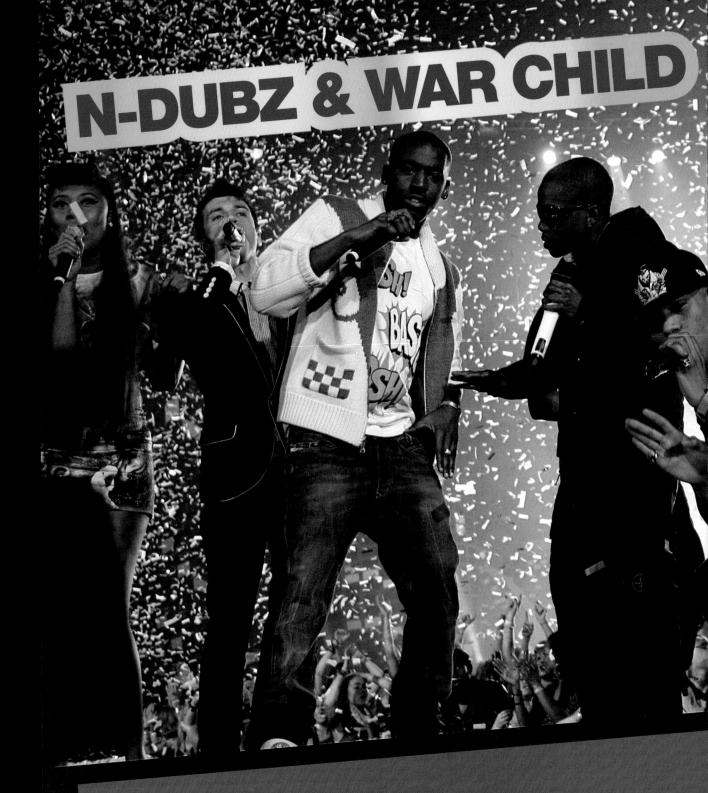

N-DUBZ & WAR CHILD

In 2009 N-Dubz were part of a super-group called The Young Soul Rebels who recorded a single for the charity War Child.

War Child helps kids in poverty in countries where wars and military conflicts have taken place.

The single was called 'I Got Soul' and was a hip hop/R&B version of the track "All these things that I've done" by The Killers. It got to number 10 in the charts and earned thousands of pounds for the charity.

As well as Dappy, Fazer and Tulisa, also on the record are N-Dubz's big mate Tinchy Stryder,

VV Brown, Pixie Lott, Frankmusik, Chipmunk, Ironik and Kid British.

The song was performed live at the 2009 MOBO Awards with Tulisa singing Pixie Lott's lines as she couldn't make it.

N-Dubz got soul!

NAME THAT TUNE

Can you fill in the gaps with the missing words in these N-Dubz song titles?

1. "Strong *again*"

2. "*Feva* Las Vegas"

3. "You Better Not *Waste* My *Time*"

4. "*Playing* With Fire"

5. "We *dance* On"

6. "Love For My *Slum*"

7. "Work *Work*"

8. "I Don't Wanna Go To *Sleep*"

9. "Say It's *over*"

10. "*Juke* Man Skit"

Answers on page 60/61

Fierce! Tulisa's Style

Tulisa reckons she's one of the most unfashionable people in the world! But N-Dublets know better, we reckon she's got a fierce style as the photos here show!

At home she prefers jeans with maybe some Ugg boots and t-shirts. When she's working hard in the studio it might be Adidas trainers and a nice comfortable tracksuit.

On stage she likes to look stylish and different but knows that with his unusual but always dapper styling, she usually has to give way to Dappy!

She says that her idea of an outfit for a night out is a nice pair of high heels, stylish leggings and maybe a corset. That, or a simple, cute girly dress with her hair up.

Despite her success she still likes to shop where she always has at Kilburn High Road or the market stalls on Camden High Street.

We think it doesn't matter what she wears or where it came from, she always looks a million Duku Dollars! Go girl!

ALL THE TUNES: THE ALBUMS

N-Dubz have achieved so much already it's hard to believe they have only made two albums!

Check them out:

First album: Uncle B

Release date: 17 November 2008

Record label: All Around The World Records

Highest chart position: 11

Tracklist:

1. "Intro"
2. "Wouldn't You"
3. "Strong Again"
4. "Don't Get Nine"
5. "I Swear"
6. "Ouch"
7. "N-Dubz vs. NAA"
8. "Public Transport (Skit)"
9. "Love For My Slum" (ft. Baker Trouble)
10. "You Better Not Waste My Time"
11. "Work Work"
12. "Feva Las Vegas"
13. "Defeat You" (ft. Chipmunk)
14. "Sex"
15. "Secrets"
16. "Papa Can You Hear Me?"
17. "Outro"

Second album: Against All Odds
Release date: 16 November 2009
Record label: All Around The World/Def Jam Records

Highest chart position: 6

Tracklist:
1. "Intro"
2. "I Need You"
3. "Playing With Fire" (ft. Mr Hudson)
4. "Say It's Over"
5. "Na Na"
6. "Shoulda Put Something On"
7. "Duku Man Skit" (ft. Fearless)
8. "I Don't Wanna Go To Sleep"
9. "Suck Yourself" (ft. Chipmunk)
10. "No One Knows"
11. "Number One" (N-Dubz Remix ft. Tinchy Stryder)
12. "Comfortable"
13. "Let Me Be" (ft. NiVo)
14. "Outro"

UNCLE B: THE MAN, THE ALBUM

Uncle B – The Main Man

'Uncle B' was Byron Contostavlos, Dappy's dad, Tulisa's uncle and the main man behind the band in their early days.

But Uncle B was also the name everyone concerned with the band used for him (especially Fazer) as he was such an inspirational figure.

'B' as he was also known was in a band himself when he was younger with his brother Steve and Steve's wife Anne - who are Tulisa's mum and dad! They were part of the band Mungo Jerry, who had a massive UK hit with a song called 'In The Summertime".

Sadly it never happened for them after that though,

so once Dappy showed he had the skills, Byron was determined to make N-Dubz a success. He had his own recording studio in Dollis Hill where N-Dubz learnt all about making great records.

Sadly Byron, who Tulisa called 'my lovely uncle', died in 2007 when N-Dubz were still making their first album. The song 'Papa, Can You Hear Me?' is Dappy's heartfelt tribute to his dad.

Uncle B – The Best-selling Award-winning Album

Uncle B is, of course, a tribute to Byron. It was released on All Around The World records in November 2008, went platinum and won the MOBO Award for best album in 2009. 'Nuff said.

STREET SMART! FAZER'S STYLE

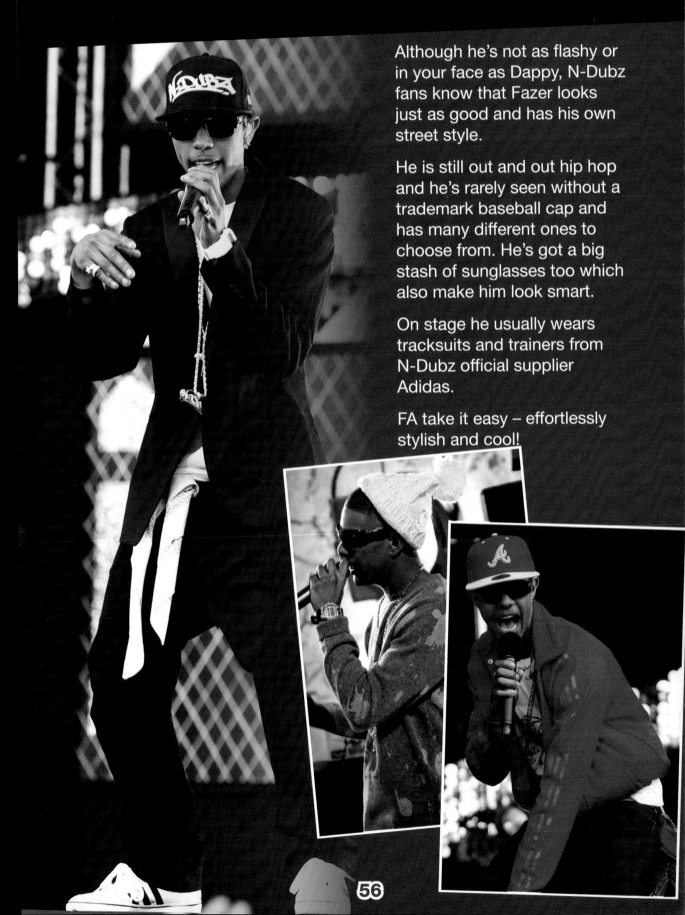

Although he's not as flashy or in your face as Dappy, N-Dubz fans know that Fazer looks just as good and has his own street style.

He is still out and out hip hop and he's rarely seen without a trademark baseball cap and has many different ones to choose from. He's got a big stash of sunglasses too which also make him look smart.

On stage he usually wears tracksuits and trainers from N-Dubz official supplier Adidas.

FA take it easy – effortlessly stylish and cool!

Dappy gets lots of headlines for his hats but he's got an original style which, like Fazer's, comes straight from the street.

His name even comes from the fact that he's a dapper young dude who always tries to stand out.

The first thing N-Dublets usually want to know when N-Dubz take the stage is what hat Dappy is wearing tonight. And, whether it's a Dappy special from Camden Market or a simple bandana, he never lets them down.

Like Fazer, he always wears Adidas on stage, as the band were specially selected to wear their trainers and clothes!

D to the A to the Ps to the Y! – the dapper young rapper, na na!

VIDEO STARZ!

N-Dubz don't just make great songs and award-winning albums they make dynamite videos too. These are some of the best:

WE DANCE ON

N-Dubz don't appear in this vid but it includes some of the best young (really young!) dancers in the UK and features Bodyrox. It's also a promo for the brilliant film Street Dance and has lots of great shots of Diversity and Flawless.

SAY IT'S OVER

Dappy, Fazer and Tulisa look great even in the future! This one starts with the band using touch screen computers on a wicked-looking spaceship, before Dappy spits lyrics about how hard it is to tell someone you want to leave them. Wait 'til you see the car Fazer is sitting on!

PLAYING WITH FIRE

This starts with some brilliant and iconic shots of all of N-Dubz and Mr Hudson in the dark with Tower Bridge in the background. As usual all of the band look fantastic in stunning outfits as various little stories play out. The night shots of London look great too. Check out Mr Hudson's vocals. Zoop Zoop!

I NEED YOU

Dappy arrives in an N-Dubz branded helicopter, Tulisa's in a flash car and Fazer arrives on his favourite mode of transport, a superbike! Just like in Playing With Fire each of the band then tells a story about meeting a beautiful boy or girl who then disappears. Must be crazy!

ANSWERS

SPOT THE DIFFERENCE (PAGE 16)

THE BIG QUIZ (PAGE 17)

1. Richard Rawson
2. Against All Odds
3. Three
4. True
5. Def Jam
6. Tinchy Stryder
7. Tula
8. Camden
9. False, it was 'Lickle Rinsers Crew'
10. 2007
11. True
12. Laurissa
13. Sleezy
14. True
15. Dubplate Drama
16. The Sun
17. Street Dance 3D
18. 2009
19. Playing With Fire
20. Dino

WORDSEARCH (PAGE 23)

```
C Q Q F F L C H C U O N N P Q
M R N R T B V K K T N B G T T
T A F L U J Y C Q L R L L Y B
R L J Z L K Z R X C Y T P X M
S K K F A M U L O T U L I S A
T W R N E Z K K N N P W N E G
E K L F W D U B V B H Y N Z N
L C N T K H D K M I P O X N L
B D K D I N O R P P R Y E D J
U R F J Y U R H A E M D L T R
D K L A N K O D B L M M Z D A
N V N C Z P N M L A M G M M P
V G L M B E U I C B M K J O A
K E P B N N R X P G K N Y B P
B Q C Q Y J N O D N O L Q O N
```

NAME THAT TUNE (PAGE 48)

1. Again
2. Feva
3. Waste / Time
4. Playing
5. Dance
6. Slum
7. Work
8. Sleep
9. Over
10. Duku

Picture Credits